# DK 24 HOURS

# Arctic

# DK

LONDON, NEW YORK, MUNICH,
MELBOURNE, and DELHI

**Written and edited by** Lorrie Mack
**Designed by** Clare Shedden

**Publishing manager** Susan Leonard
**Art director** Rachael Foster
**Category publisher** Mary Ling
**Picture researchers** Julia Harris-Voss
and Jo Walton
**Production** Lucy Baker
**DTP designers** Emma Hansen-Knarhoi
and Ben Hung
**Jacket editor** Mariza O'Keeffe
**Jacket designer** Mary Sandberg
**Jacket copywriter** Adam Powley

**Consultants** Bryan and Cherry Alexander

First published in Great Britain in 2007 by
Dorling Kindersley Limited
80 Strand, London WC2R 0RL

A CIP catalogue record for this book
is available from the British Library.

ISBN 978-1-40531-622-4

Colour reproduction by Colourscan, Singapore
Printed and bound by
L. Rex Printing Co. Ltd, China

Discover more at
**www.dk.com**

# Welcome to the Arctic, the

**4:00 am** Dawn

**10:00 am** Morning

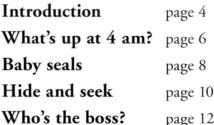

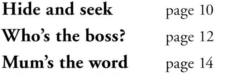

The Arctic is not only very very **cold** –
the air is as dry as a **desert**.

# icy, remote land at the very top of the world.

**2:00 pm** Afternoon

**6:00 pm** Dusk

**10:00 pm** Night

Most of the **Arctic** is a big frozen sea with a few areas of land around the edges. Come and spend 24 hours with the animals who live there.

In most of the world, each 24-hour period is part day, part night – long days in summer, long nights in winter. At the poles, though, there is no dark night in summer, and no bright day in winter. *24 Hours Arctic* takes you through an April day with the animals who live there.

The Arctic is a huge ocean. It used to be ice covered all year round, but as the Earth gets warmer, more and more of it is thawing.

## Walrus

With their huge bodies, walruses are clumsy and comical on land or ice. They spend two-thirds of their life in water, though, where they move quickly and gracefully, powered by flat flippers that act like big paddles.

## Polar bear

Like walruses, polar bears are natural swimmers who can stay in freezing water for hours. Also like walruses, they have a thick layer of fat to keep them warm. The polar bear is the biggest bear on Earth.

# Snowy owl

Snowy owls are one of the few birds who live in the Arctic all year. When they nest, their chicks can all be different ages, since the mother starts hatching each egg as soon as it's laid. If food is scarce, the big chicks eat the little ones.

Throughout the book, these little shapes will appear with outlines of different creatures to give you an idea of how big the animals are. Our guide shapes are based on children about 115cm (3 ft 9 in) tall.

**Summer sun on Arctic lands**

North Pole

night

day

Earth's axis

South Pole

For much of the year, Arctic days are either all light or all dark. This is because the Earth's axis (an imaginary line through the centre) is tilted toward the Sun in summer, so its rays shine on the Arctic full time; the Sun never reaches the Arctic in winter. So, while animals in the rest of the world do things (like eat and sleep) at particular times of day, Arctic creatures can do almost any thing at almost any time.

# Arctic deer

In the Canadian Arctic, these animals are called caribou, and they are wild. In north Europe, they are often domesticated, and the term reindeer is used. Whatever their name, there are more of them in the Arctic than any other large mammal.

# Arctic fox

Although they look much like other foxes, Arctic foxes have slightly shorter legs, tails, ears, and muzzles. This difference helps protect them from the bitter cold because it means there is less surface area exposed to it.

**1** Harp seal pup

A**t dawn,** the short night begins to lift. At this time of year nights are dusky but never really dark, because the Sun doesn't set completely. All by himself on the shadowy ice, a harp seal pup lies resting and waiting for his mother to deliver his next meal.

Using his keen sense of smell, a **polar bear** stalks prey. If there's a seal breathing hole nearby, he has a good chance of catching his supper.

There's nothing like a horny hoof and a big pair of antlers when a **caribou** needs to scratch himself in hard-to-reach places.

This **Arctic fox** is tucking into the carcass of a bird he has killed. If he can't eat it all, some other hungry creature will finish the leftovers.

To pull his huge body out of the water and onto an ice floe, this basking **walrus** uses his long pointed tusks as levers.

Unlike other owls, **snowies** don't sleep in the day and hunt at night. They usually set out to find prey around dawn and dusk.

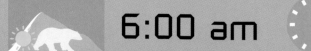 

# Plentiful in Arctic seas,

harp seals are hugely sociable, living and travelling together in big, noisy groups. They **gather** on floating ice floes far from shore, and **dive** for small fish in deep water. Harp-seal pups, born in late **winter**, are still very young in April.

Mother harp seals touch noses with their pups as a greeting, and to identify them as their own.

Because of their pale fur, new babies are called "whitecoats".

When they're first born, pups feed on their mum's rich milk. Soon they have a thick layer of blubber to keep them warm.

Two female seals both think this young pup is their own. If they can't sort things out, there's likely to be a fight.

These two are still youngsters, but their white fur has fallen out and a thinner, grey, adult coat has taken its place.

### Ice, ice babies

Just before giving birth (called whelping), female harp seals haul themselves onto winter pack ice in their thousands. An area of ice where pups are born and nursed by their mothers is called a whelping patch.

For their first two weeks, pups just lie on the ice and wait for their mums to come and feed them. Their thick white fur keeps them warm.

9

**Many Arctic** animals are white so they can't be seen in the snow. This natural disguise, called camouflage, conceals some creatures from predators and allows others to attack before they're spotted by prey.

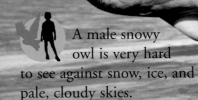

A male snowy owl is very hard to see against snow, ice, and pale, cloudy skies.

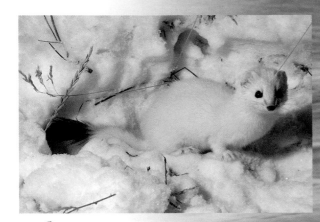

Ermines are a kind of stoat, and, like all stoats, they have a black tail tip, even when the rest of their fur is white. If hungry birds spot this, and swoop down to nip it, the ermine can pull away quickly.

Arctic wolves are closely related to ordinary grey wolves. One big difference, though, is their colouring – they are always pale. This snarling creature is almost pure white, but Arctic wolves are sometimes cream or light grey.

# Hide and seek

Look closely at this scene and you'll find a winter-white ptarmigan perched in the snow. In summer, this bird has speckled brown or grey feathers.

As well as keeping him warm, the white fur coat on this baby seal makes it very hard for predators to spot him lying on the snow and ice.

**Arctic hares** are not just white in winter – they're white all year round, but in summer they have a slightly greyish hue. The biggest of all hares, they dig for food under the snow.

Bigger than an Arctic fox, an Arctic hare has huge feet, and can reach speeds of 40 mph (65 kph).

11

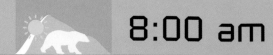 

Apart from humans, there are no animals in the Arctic that hunt polar bears. As well as being the biggest bear in the world, this creature is the unchallenged ruler of the northern landscape.

**Lone wanderer**

With the exception of females with cubs, polar bears mostly live and hunt alone. They spend much of their lives on sea ice, hunting seals. Males are about twice as big as females; they weigh up to 650 kg (1400 lbs) – as much as ten people.

12

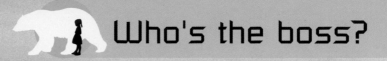

**Bear behaviour**

A polar bear's sense of smell is much better than yours or mine – he can sniff a seal from several miles (kilometres) away.

## Home is where the hunt is

Polar bears live in areas where there is a mix of land ice, sea ice, and sea. In spring, males spend about a quarter of their time hunting. When they're not hunting, they're sleeping or resting.

These young males may look as if they're having a vicious battle. But, like many other animals, they just enjoying play fighting.

Like humans, polar bears walk on the soles of their feet, putting their heels down first.

With their warm fur and thick layer of blubber, polar bears get overheated very easily. Sometimes a rest is the best thing.

13

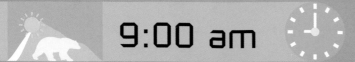

## 9:00 am

**Female polar bears** take care of their cubs until they're two or three years old – **fathers** aren't involved at all. Mums give birth (usually to two babies) in a den, and they don't come out until the cubs are several **months** old.

### Safe at home

Cubs are born in the middle of winter, but they stay in their den until March or April. Before mums give birth, they have to store enough fat to nourish themselves for all that time, and to provide milk for their babies as well.

Watched by one of her babies, this mum enjoys being out in the open after her long months in the den.

Dens are usually in snow, but they can be dug out of snow-covered earth as well.

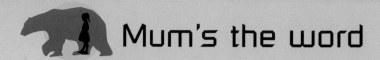

**Life lessons**

Cubs begin eating solid food as soon as Mum makes her first kill. After they're about a year old, they'll have learned to hunt from watching her.

.... Hungry birds such as gulls hang around for leftovers.

**9:10 am** Mum and her cubs eat and eat until they're stuffed. Nobody cares if they make a big mess.

**9:50 am** Phew! Three full tummies! Mum decides that breakfast time is over, and calls her babies to join her in the water.

**9:54 am** Bears do most of their hunting on frozen bits of sea, so they're very good swimmers. Now they'll head home for a good rest.

Mums often make dens in big snowdrifts along the coast.

**1** Walrus

T he Arctic sky is very bright by 10:00 in the morning. A lone walrus, tired of sunning himself on an ice floe, lowers his body back into the sea. The visible splash is made by one of his back flippers, which propel him through the water.

Being able to break ice with his front paws is a very important hunting skill for a **polar bear.** Who knows? He might find food underneath.

There's still snow on the ground, so **reindeer** use their hooves and snouts to get at food underneath it. Mosses and lichens are particular favourites.

Male **Arctic foxes** usually hunt alone. They can cover huge distances – up to 1000 km (620 m) – in one journey looking for food.

**Walruses** are happy in water, and they're excellent swimmers. Like all his family, this one can stay submerged for up to half an hour.

Female **snowy owls** are a bit bigger than males, and flecked all over with brown. Males are mostly white with a few flecks on their chest and tail.

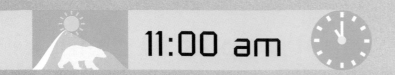

# With their chubby cheeks and button nose, **walruses** look quite cuddly. Big males are hard to cuddle, though – at 3.5 m (4 yds) long, and 1700 kg (3750 lbs), they are the **size** of a small car.

Walruses are mammals, so they breathe air like we do.
This one is swimming and breathing out at the same time.

Males love to bask together in the sun. This group has gathered on pack ice in the sea.

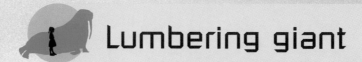

Walruses graze on the sea bed for clams, sea cucumbers, and whelks. They live in shallow water so they can reach the surface to breathe.

Male walruses (or bulls) put on noisy displays of aggression. While they don't fight with their sharp tusks, these can cause injury accidentally. Some experts think they help to locate food.

Although they spend two thirds of their life in the water, walruses sometimes surface and rest on ice floes.

Under their wrinkly skin, walruses have a layer of fat (called **blubber**) about 10 cm (4 in) thick.

## Feeding faces

Both male and female walruses have tusks and moustache whiskers. They use their snouts and their sensitive whiskers to feel for food on the ocean floor, then get at it by squirting water from their mouth to loosen tasty morsels, and digging them out with their snout.

**Lots of animals** spend time under the sea. Even though it's freezing cold there, it's quite a bit warmer than the Arctic air, and there are lots of delicious fish to eat.

Narwhals are a type of small whale. The males have a single, straight tusk with spiral grooves along its length. Like a walrus tusk, this is actually a long tooth. Many historians think it inspired the myth of the unicorn.

As well as swimming, walruses can also sleep underwater. To do this, they fill sacs in their throat with air. These act like floats, allowing the creatures to bob up and down while they snooze.

**Pure white** with smiley mouths, beluga whales have sharp teeth for eating fish and squid. Because they're small and a bit slow, belugas are eaten by bigger whales – and even by polar bears.

Harp seal babies start to swim and catch fish to eat when they're only about four weeks old.

Seals move through the water by stroking alternately with their two back flippers.

Plankton, the main food of baleen whales, contains millions of tiny plants and animals.

Among the chief foods in plankton are long, red, shrimp-like creatures called krill.

The "whalebone" that used to stiffen corsets is actually baleen from whales.

Unlike narwhals and belugas, bowhead whales have no teeth. They filter plankton from vast amounts of water passing through a big fibrous fringe (baleen) in their mouth.

21

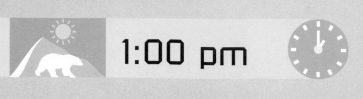
# Along Arctic shores, sheets

of sea ice are firmly attached to the land.
The place where this ice meets the open
water – called the floe edge – attracts lots
of animals and birds.

From the floe edge, polar bears can dive
into the sea for safety if they sense danger.

Eiders are "diving
ducks"– they dive
in the water for
seafood and fish.

During late spring and
summer, there are lots
of birds around the
floe edge. This duck is
called a spectacled eider
– can you guess why?

**The floe edge moves** with the seasons.
In the winter, it's at its furthest point from
land. Then, when the sea ice begins to melt
in spring, the floe edge moves further and
further in. Wind, waves, and
currents also wear it away.

Scavenging birds such as these ravens follow the floe edge for food. Many ravens not only breed in the Arctic, they spend all winter there.

Sea mammals feed on fish, seafood, and plants at the floe edge. This bow whale is filtering plankton through the baleen fringe in its mouth.

Some floe-edge waters are rich in shrimp and clams. This bearded seal's head is red from the high iron content of the mud where he digs for these tasty creatures.

Common guillemots feed underwater on small schools of fish, crustaceans, worms, and squid. They can dive up to 50m (165 ft) deep.

There are plenty of walrus at the floe edge when it's close to their shallow feeding grounds.

23

1 Little auks

**M**id-afternoon, and the sky is full of little auks (also called dovekies). They breed in huge numbers in the spring, laying their eggs in sheltered holes and crevices in slopes or cliffs overlooking the sea.

Happy paddling through icy water, a hungry **polar bear** travels from one ice floe to another in search of a plump fish or marine mammal to eat.

Since they've broken into a gallop, these **caribou** have probably been startled, or they sense danger lurking near their herd.

To pounce on his prey hiding in the snow (a vole or a lemming, maybe), this **Arctic fox** springs high up into the air.

**Walruses** have thick, rough, very wrinkly skin covered with short, coarse hair. They are usually a dark greyish-brown colour.

A **snowy owl** cruises the sky looking for lemmings to eat. If there are plenty, these birds live in the Arctic all year. If not, they go south in winter.

25

# Some Arctic birds, like snowy owls, ptarmigans, ravens, and some guillemots, live there all year round; they are called residents. Others, such as geese, ducks, and terns, fly there to breed during the summer months; these birds are known as migrants.

The Arctic tern completes a spectacular migration every year – it flies 35,400 km (22,000 m) to the Antarctic and back again!

Eider ducks are migrants. They eat mostly shellfish – especially clams, which they crush with their strong bills and swallow whole.

Long-tailed (oldsquaw) ducks, which are very common in the Arctic, have dramatic brown-and-white colouring. They make a lot of noise calling to each other.

Arctic terns live and breed in large groups called colonies.

When they're not breeding, common guillemots travel over or under the sea to find food. This one is doing his under-water flying trick.

Every so often, every bird in the colony suddenly goes quiet, then – all at once – they all fly away. This phenomenon is known as the "dread".

Snow geese are white, with half-black wings. They breed in the Arctic, but they don't live there all year round.

Beside a glacier, a tern colony breeds and feeds alongside fulmars and kittiwakes, other Arctic birds that get nearly all their food from the sea.

Check out our cool black-and-white **feather** coats.

**Brünnich's guillemots** (or thick-billed mürres) breed on rocky cliffs in huge, smelly, noisy, colonies. These birds are strong fliers, but clumsy on take-off and landing. In fact, they move more easily through water than air.

27

The furry lemming occupies a very important place in the Arctic food chain — at the very bottom. Every one of the region's meat-eating mammals and birds see him as a snack. For some, like foxes and snowy owls, he's their main diet, while others turn to lemmings when bigger, meatier prey is not available.

Long-tailed jaegers feed mainly on lemmings; sometimes they steal them from other birds. They even dig in the ground to get into the lemmings' burrows.

I eat mostly **plants**, but I can manage the odd **insect** too.

**Because the lemming** is a staple food for so many other creatures, animal communities in the Arctic depend on his existence. So, when the lemmings' food is scarce and their numbers fall, the other wildlife suffers as well.

"Please don't see me!"

Collared lemmings grow long winter claws on their front feet so they can dig through the snow for their food.

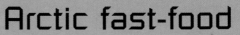

Gyrfalcons need lemmings – when there are lots of lemmings, there are lots of gyrfalcons too.

Snowy owls eat mostly lemmings, so when there aren't enough of them, snowy numbers drop dramatically.

Ermines may look sweet to us, but lemmings and voles – their chief prey – are terrified of them.

The powerful Arctic wolf really prefers caribou or musk oxen to eat, but when there aren't any around, he'll settle for seals, ducks, hares – or lemmings.

Small mammals in general – and lemmings in particular – make up the Arctic fox's diet.

Lemmings are a great favourite with the wolverine, but it will eat other small animals – and some very big ones too!

29

# Mighty musk oxen are the only Arctic creatures who never need to seek shelter, no matter how **bitter** and **blizzardy** it gets. Their name comes from the strong **scent** the males develop during the mating season.

*This scary formation is*

**Coat of many layers**

Each musk ox has a covering of coarse, shaggy hair (called guard hair) that hangs down like a long skirt over its stocky body. Underneath this are fine, soft hairs that provide lightweight insulation.

30

## Communal living

This very new calf has bumps where his horns will grow and a coat of short guard hair. Sometimes he keeps warm under his mother's skirt.

Because they're being threatened (probably by wolves or a polar bear), these adults form a circle facing outward, with the youngsters safe inside.

called a "defensive ring"

**5:02 pm** Once snow falls, it forms a crust that lasts until the thaw. In winter, oxen use their hooves to get at the lichen and grass they like to eat.

**5:14 pm** Adults can run as fast as 25 mph (40 kph). They move fast to escape enemies, and youngsters like to chase each other just for fun.

**5:45 pm** These males are "jousting" – facing off, backing away, then running at each other and head-butting. They will do this until one gives up.

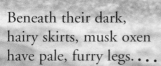

Beneath their dark, hairy skirts, musk oxen have pale, furry legs.

31

**1** Reindeer

**S**ince they've spent the winter in the barren Arctic, these reindeer are very thin, but this may not be due to starvation. Some experts think that when winter approaches, reindeer instinctively eat less to reduce their weight. As a result, they don't need so much food to survive.

Despite being well fed and fat, this **polar bear** has killed a seal. He may eat only its skin and fat, but a hungry bear would strip the bones.

**Caribou** don't live in the very coldest part of the Arctic, but they wander quite far north in spring, when the females (called cows) have their babies.

When a blizzard threatens, this **Arctic fox** protects his face from the cold by wrapping his thick, bushy tail right around his body.

**Walruses** grunt very loudly when they're fighting or irritated. When a group gathers together, the racket can be heard miles away.

When a **snowy owl** captures prey, she hides it from other hunters by tucking it under her wing. This behaviour is called "mantling".

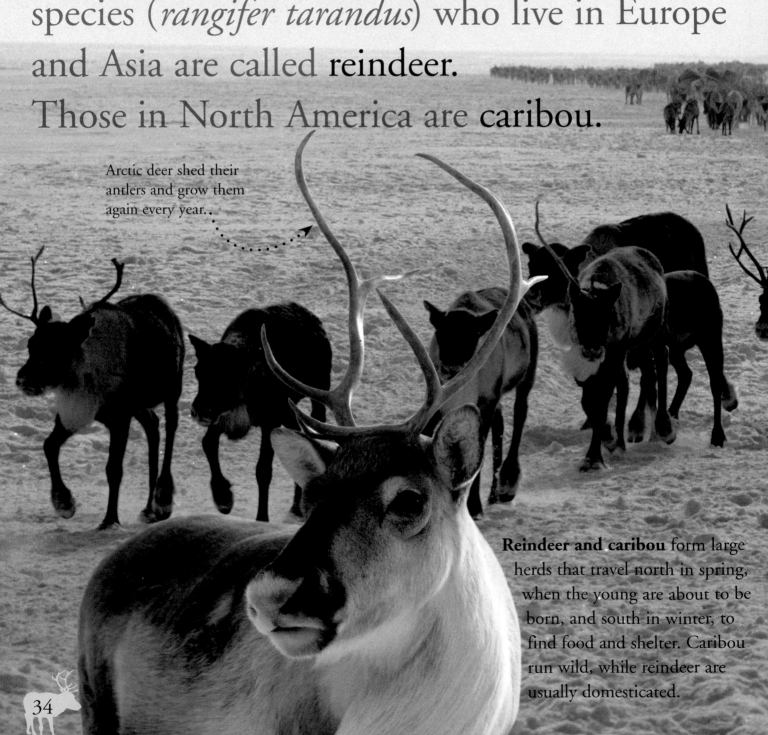

**Arctic deer** migrate long distances, their hooves are adapted for snow, and males and females both have **antlers**. Members of this species (*rangifer tarandus*) who live in Europe and Asia are called **reindeer**. Those in North America are **caribou**.

Arctic deer shed their antlers and grow them again every year.

**Reindeer and caribou** form large herds that travel north in spring, when the young are about to be born, and south in winter, to find food and shelter. Caribou run wild, while reindeer are usually domesticated.

34

Arctic deer (like this caribou) use their hooves and snouts to get at grasses and lichens under the crusty snow.

Both caribou and reindeer migrate huge distances (up to 1000 km, 622 miles), but reindeer like these are usually accompanied by native human herders.

An Arctic deer's hooves help him to paddle in water and walk on snow. These caribou are crossing a river on the route of their autumn migration.

### Survival of the fiercest

Jaegers are large, aggressive seabirds that eat small mammals, fish, and other birds. This one is tucking into a tasty ptarmigan.

Having hunted and killed a baby hare, this Arctic fox is about to eat him up.

Ferocious wolverines are capable of killing mammals much larger than they are. This one is feeding on a caribou carcass.

# To us, the Arctic seems a harsh and cruel place where food is scarce. Many animals survive by hunting, killing, and eating other creatures – a way of life that is common in nature. Animals that do this are known as predators.

Wolves cover huge distances across open icescapes in their search for food.

There's nothing a polar bear likes more than a delicious seal supper on sea ice.

36

This pack of wolves is chasing a herd of hairy musk oxen at high speed.

**The Arctic wolf** will hunt and kill more or less any creatures he can find – small ones like ptarmigan, hares, and lemmings if they're around, or big musk oxen and caribou if necessary.

37

**When you go outside** in the winter, you wear special shoes or boots to keep your feet warm and to stop you from slipping on ice and snow. In the Arctic, animal feet need the same protection as yours would, so nature has provided special adaptations for the harsh environment.

A reindeer's toes spread out, acting like snowshoes to distribute his weight over a wide patch of snow or ice. The feet stay flexible because they're full of soft, fatty tissue.

**The Arctic hare's long,** silky, white fur covers his whole body, including his legs and feet. In the bitterest cold, hares sit on their back feet, which are insulated with particularly thick, coarse, yellowish fur.

For grip, Arctic hares have clawed toes – four on the back paws and five on the front paws.

When they walk across pack ice, polar bears leave clear tracks. These are quite fresh, so the bear can't be far away!··········

The ptarmigan's thick feathers reach the tips of his toes to protect him from cold. During the winter, feathers cover even the soles of his feet to enhance his grip.

Even though you can't see them, there are hundreds of tiny, wart-like bumps on the bottom a walrus fin. These help the huge creature to grip onto slippery ice floes.

Humans, polar bears' only predators, use their tracks to hunt them.

Polar bears have thick, black, hairless, bumpy pads on the soles and toes of their paws. There are five clawed toes on each paw, with long hair in between.

1 Polar bear

At night time in April, Arctic light is soft, pinkish, and dim. The sun is still in the sky, even though it's very low, so animals don't necessarily sleep. Lone polar bears like this one may hunt now, moving slowly and stealthily across large expanses of ice.

When **a polar bear** yawns, you can see that his nose, mouth, and tongue are black. Underneath his white fur, his skin is black too.

In Norway, herds containing thousands of **reindeer** are moving north for the summer – they even travel in heavy snowstorms.

This **Arctic fox's** thick winter coat keeps him cosy. In the summer, his fur is not only a different colour – greyish brown – it's much finer too.

**Walrus** tusks, which are actually long teeth, help to define a male's status within a group. The ones with big tusks tend to be the leaders.

A **Snowy owl's** big eyes are incredibly powerful – he can see well in the dark, and he can also spot prey on the ground from high in the sky.

# Food can be scarce in the

Arctic, so some animals eat what other animals leave behind from a kill. They also feed on the bodies of creatures that have died naturally, or even on human rubbish. Occasionally – when starvation threatens – they go even further ...

 A hungry wolf sniffs shed antlers in hope of finding a shred of flesh to chew on.

Polar bears strip **whale bones** completely clean – of skin and **blubber** as well as flesh.

Scavenging means eating dead animals or human rubbish.

**Washed up on an Arctic beach,** the carcass of a bowhead whale attracts scavenging polar bears. Although we think of seals as their main food, some experts believe that up to ten per cent of their diet is made of whale meat.

Glaucous gulls are very large birds.

 Ravens are skilled scavengers who are often found picking at the carcasses of seals and caribou.

It's not only polar bears who eat seals. Glaucous gulls can't kill seals, but they scavenge on dead ones.

On land, Arctic foxes can be found hanging around polar bears. When food is very, very scarce, they sometimes eat bears' droppings.

Wolverines are well suited to scavenging – their powerful jaws and strong neck muscles allow them to crush bones and bite through frozen flesh.

## Animals who spend

their lives in the Arctic use up
lots of energy just keeping warm,
as well as moving around finding
food. They need plenty of rest, but
because there aren't always light days
with dark nights here, they sleep
whenever they feel like it.

This sleepy fox tucks his wet nose under his tail for warmth.

Arctic foxes often wake up late in the evening, since they tend to spend all night hunting for lemmings. When they sleep, they curl themselves into tight balls.

In April, the **Arctic** can still be colder than your home **freezer.**

**A big slab of sea ice** may seem a funny place to lie
down for a nap, but walruses are quite comfortable
there. They don't have soft fur like polar bears or
foxes, but their blubber is so thick and warm that
they can sleep soundly on the coldest, hardest bed.

44

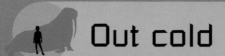 

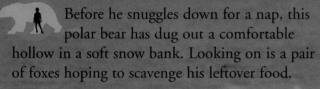 Before he snuggles down for a nap, this polar bear has dug out a comfortable hollow in a soft snow bank. Looking on is a pair of foxes hoping to scavenge his leftover food.

Having just made their way through a fierce Arctic snowstorm, a herd of migrating reindeer settles into the fresh snow for a much-needed snooze.

The walruses in the middle of this cosy spoon-fashion group are adults. The ones at the ends, with smaller tusks, are youngsters.

# From dawn to dusk

Here are some of the creatures

Snowy owl

Raven

Arctic wolf

Arctic hare

Reindeer

Arctic fox

Polar bear

Wolverine

Ptarmigans

## Glossary

Here are the meanings of some of the important words you will come across as you read about the Arctic and the animals who live there.

**BALEEN** The long fringe made of keratin (like finger nails) that some whales have in their mouth to filter plankton from the water.

**BLUBBER** The thick layer of fat that some animals (like seals) have to protect them from cold.

**BREED** To produce babies.

**BURROW** A hole in the ground that an animal lives in. Lemmings live in burrows.

**CARCASS** The dead body of an animal.

**COLONY** A group of animals that live together. Arctic terns and guillemots live in colonies.

**DEN** A safe resting place dug out of earth or snow by a wild, usually predatory, animal. Female polar bears make dens.

**FREEZING** What happens when water turns into solid ice.

**HERD** A large group of animals such as caribou that live and travel together.

**HOOVES** The curved, horny feet on some animals. Reindeer and musk oxen have hooves.

**ICE** Water that gets so cold it freezes solid.

**ICE FLOE** A flat piece of floating sea ice.

**INSULATION** Material used to keep warmth or cold (or even sound) in one place. Blubber provides insulation from cold.

**MAMMAL** A warm-blooded animal that drinks its mother's milk when it's a baby.

**MARINE** Something connected with the sea. Seals and whales are marine mammals.

**MIGRATION** Moving from one place to another according to the seasons. Animals usually migrate to breed or find food.

**NATIVE** Animals, plants, or people that belong in a particular place. Polar bears are native to the Arctic.

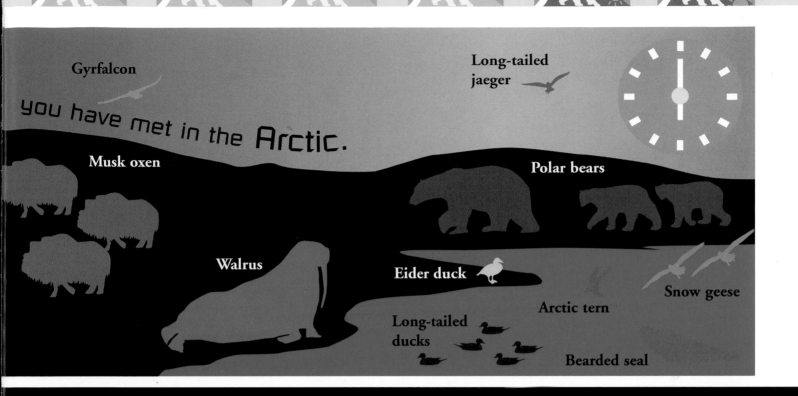

... you have met in the Arctic.

Gyrfalcon

Long-tailed jaeger

Musk oxen

Polar bears

Walrus

Eider duck

Snow geese

Arctic tern

Long-tailed ducks

Bearded seal

---

**PACK ICE** The large masses of ice that result when the frozen sea breaks up.

**PLANKTON** The mass of tiny plants and animals that float around in the sea and provide food for fish and marine animals.

**PREDATOR** An animal that hunts, kills, and eats other animals.

**PREY** An animal that is hunted, killed, and eaten by a predator.

**SCAVENGER** An animal that feeds on the carcasses of other animals, or on human rubbish.

**WHELPING PATCH** A sheet of pack ice where a large group of female seals gather to give birth to their pups.

## Picture credits

The publisher would like to thank the following for their kind permission to reproduce their photographs:

(Key: a-above; b-below/bottom; c-centre; f-far; l-left; r-right; t-top)

**Alamy Images:** Arco Images 29br, 38tc, 42tr; Juniors Bildarchiv 13tr, 31tr, 31br; blickwinkel 19tr, 28tr, 33crb; Steve Bloom Images 3, 5c, 14-15, 40, 40-41; Bryan And Cherry Alexander Photography 3, 7tr, 17tl, 18-19c, 22tr, 24, 24-25, 35br, 43tr, 43cr; Mark Duffy 7br; David Fleetham 20tl; Image State 13cr; Steven J. Kazlowski 17tr, 18-19, 19br, 25cr, 30bl, 31tl, 36tl, 36clb, 41tr, 41crb, 42-43; Marco Regalia 35tr; John Schwieder 14bl; D.Kjaer / The National Trust Photo Library 26tl; Visual & Written SL 4br, 5br, 23tr, 29tl, 29cr; **AlaskaStock.com:** (c) 2006 Steven Kazlowski 12bl; Gary Schultz 1; Ardea: Sid Roberts 10tl; Jack Swedberg 33cra; M. Watson 11tl; Doc White 17crb; Andrey Zvoznikor 28bl; **Bryan and Cherry Alexander Photography:** 4tl, 22bl, 22-23, 26bl, 30-31b, 31cr, 38-39, 45tl; **Corbis:** Theo Allofs 17cr; Tom Brakefield 36cla; Tom Brakefield / Zefa 8bl; Alan & Sandy Carey / Zefa 10bl; Philip James Corwin 20cr; Daniel J. Cox 48; Dan Guravich 4bl, 8-9, 9tr; Hannu Hautala / Frank Lane Picture Agency 5bl; Jacques Langevin / Sygma 37t (background); George D. Lepp 41cr; Frank Lukasseck / Zefa 2, 6, 6-7; Hans Reinhard / Zefa 3, 32, 32tl, 32-33; Sea World of California 20b; Uwe Walz 43tl; Stuart Westmorland 27br; Staffon Widstrand 29bl; Douglas Wilson / FLPA 21cl; Winifried Wisniewski /

Zefa 5tl; **FLPA:** Ron Austing 25br; Jim Brandenburgh / Minden Pictures 5tr, 12, 25cra, 36-37, 37t, 37b; Flip de Nooyer / Foto Natura 26cl, FLIP Nicklin / Minden PIctures 21b, 23bl, 39br; Michio Hoshino / Minden Pictures 13br; David Hosking 26-27; Yva Momatiuk / John Eastcott / Minden Pictures 35tl, 37tl; Michael Quinton / Minden Pictures 23tl; Rinie Van Muers / Foto Natura 44-45; John Watkins 26clb; Winifried Wisniewski 27tr; Winifried Wisniewski / Foto Natura 10tr; Konrad Wothe / Minden Pictures 29tr; **Getty Images:** Pal Hermansen 25tr; National Geographic 2-3b; **Magnus Elander:** 2, 10-11, 15t, 15cl, 15c, 15cr, 16tl, 16-17, 19tl, 38bl, 39tr, 39cr; **naturepl.com:** Doug Allan 23cr; Terry Andrewartha 7cr; Niall Benvie 17br; Asgeir Helgestad 17cra, 41cra, 45tr; Steve Kazlowski 7cra; Tom Mangelsen 7crb, 29cra; Mark Payne-Gill 44tr; Mike Potts 28-29; Doc White 23br; Andrey Zvoznikov 33br; **OSF / photolibrary:** Doug Allen 21t; Daniel Cox 43br; Mark Hamblin 34bl; Norbert Rosing 11tr; **Science Photo Library:** E.R. Degginger 41br; Still Pictures: Kelvin Aitken 25crb; Kevin Schafer 18tr; **SuperStock:** age foto stock 33tr

All other images © Dorling Kindersley
For further information see: www.dkimages.com

## Acknowledgements

**Dorling Kindersley would like to thank:**
Tory Gordon-Harris, Clare Harris, Carrie Love, and Penny Smith for editorial assistance.

# Index